T0197403

Jeannie Gray

These Little Hands

AuthorHouse™
1663 Liberty Drive
Bloomington, IN 47403
www.authorhouse.com
Phone: 833-262-8899

Because of the dynamic nature of the Internet, any web addresses or links contained in this book may have changed since publication and may no longer be valid. The views expressed in this work are solely those of the author and do not necessarily reflect the views of the publisher, and the publisher hereby disclaims any responsibility for them.

Any people depicted in stock imagery provided by Getty Images are models, and such images are being used for illustrative purposes only. Certain stock imagery © Getty Images.

This book is printed on acid-free paper.

ISBN: 978-1-6655-2989-1 (sc)
ISBN: 978-1-6655-2990-7 (e)

Print information available on the last page.

Published by AuthorHouse 07/07/2021

authorHOUSE®

These
Little Hands

These little hands were
made with love.

Simply, because, these

little hands were made

by God above.

These little hands will

make many things.

These little hands will help
you fulfill your dreams.

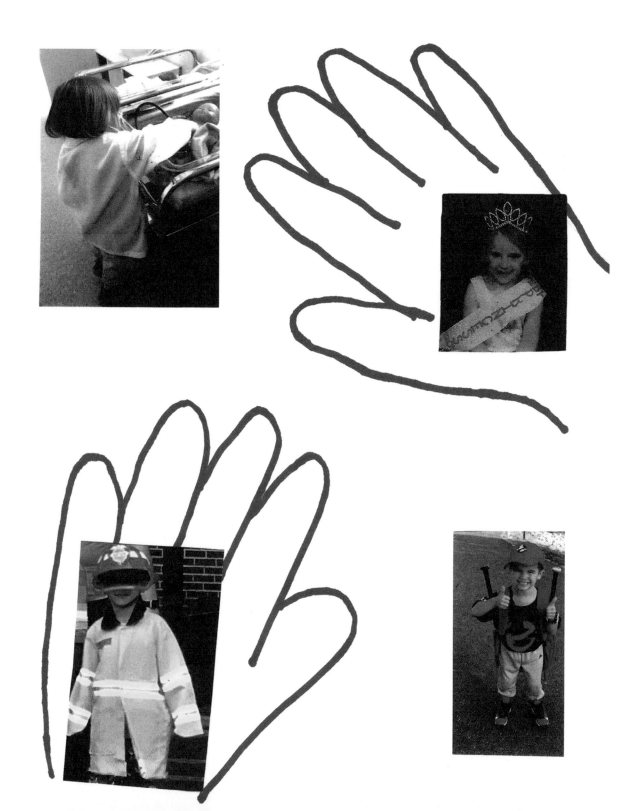

These little hands were
made just for you.

Ariyahnna
Marie Eakes

With these little hands

you will reach for all

the things you see.

These little hands will

cover your eyes.

These little hands will

reach for the skys.

These little hands

will hold a ball.

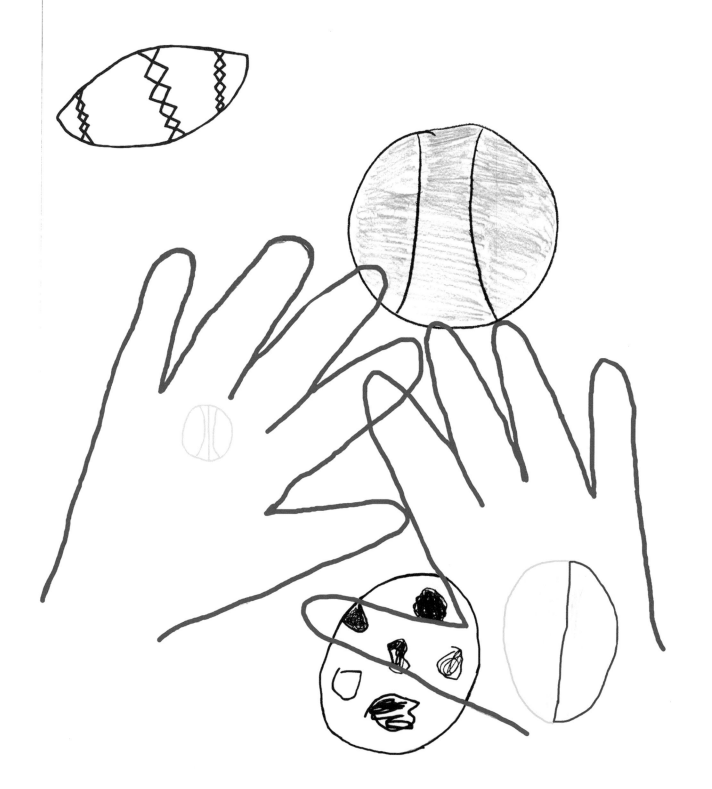

One day these little hands
will help you crawl.

These little hands, one
day you will trace.

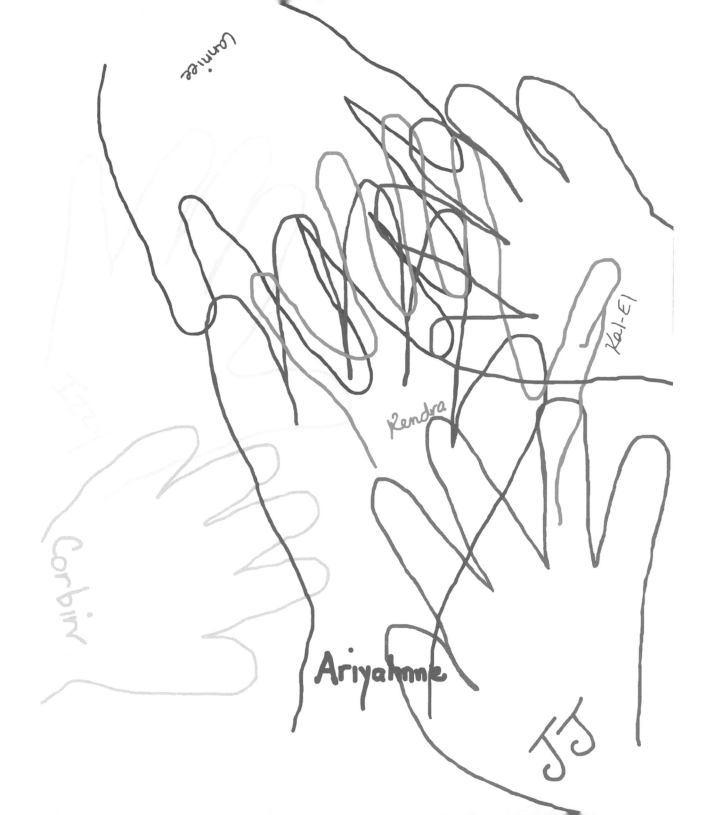

These hands will
rub your face,

These little hands will one day learn to say **HEY**.

Because these little hands
are growing day to day.

So, Mommy and Daddy, will hold these hands as much as they can.

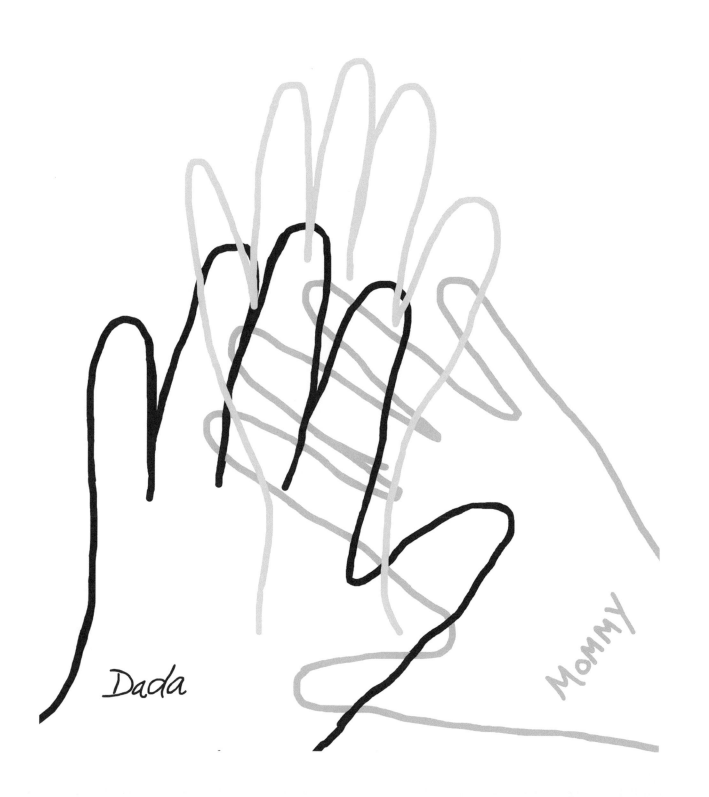

Dada

Mommy

Because one day these hands,

won't be such little hands.

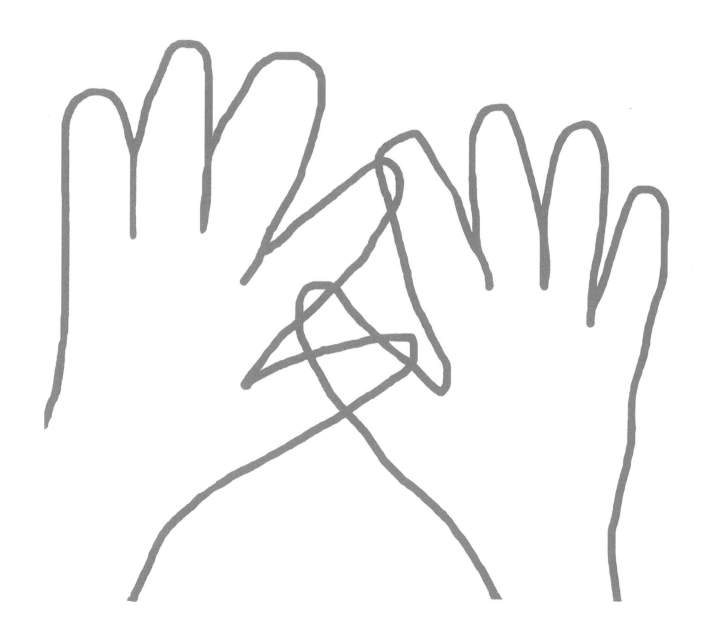

Printed in the United States
by Baker & Taylor Publisher Services